WORLD CULTURES

POLYNESIANS

CHRISTINE WEBSTER

MEDIA ENHANCED BOOKS
AV2
BY WEIGL™
ADDED VALUE • AUDIO VISUAL

www.av2books.com

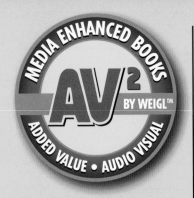

AV² provides enriched content that supplements and complements this book. Weigl's AV² books strive to create inspired learning and engage young minds in a total learning experience.

Your AV² Media Enhanced books come alive with...

Audio
Listen to sections of the book read aloud.

Key Words
Study vocabulary, and complete a matching word activity.

Go to **www.av2books.com**, and enter this book's unique code.

Video
Watch informative video clips.

Quizzes
Test your knowledge.

BOOK CODE

V 4 3 4 3 9 7

Embedded Weblinks
Gain additional information for research.

Slide Show
View images and captions, and prepare a presentation.

AV² by Weigl brings you media enhanced books that support active learning.

Try This!
Complete activities and hands-on experiments.

... and much, much more!

Published by AV² by Weigl
350 5th Avenue, 59th Floor
New York, NY 10118 USA
Website: www.weigl.com   www.av2books.com

Library of Congress Cataloging-in-Publication Data

Webster, Christine.
Polynesians / Christine Webster.
   p. cm. -- (World cultures)
Includes index.
ISBN 978-1-61913-172-9 (hard cover : alk. paper) -- ISBN 978-1-61913-533-8 (soft cover : alk. paper)
1. Polynesians--Juvenile literature. I. Title.
 GN670.W43 2012
 305.89'94--dc23
                              2011051104

Printed in the United States of America in North Mankato, Minnesota.
1 2 3 4 5 6 7 8 9 0   16 15 14 13 12

062012
WEP170512

Senior Editor Heather Kissock
Design Terry Paulhus

Consultants
Dr. Mike Evans, Professor of Anthropology

Photo Credits
Weigl acknowledges Getty Images and Alamy as primary photo suppliers for this title.

CONTENTS

2 AV² Book Code

4 Where in the World?

6 Stories and Legends

8 Out of the Past

10 Social Structures

12 Communication

14 Law and Order

16 Celebrating Culture

18 Art and Culture

20 Dressing Up

22 Food and Fun

24 Great Ideas

26 At Issue

28 Into the Future

30 World Cultures Quiz!

31 Key Words/Index

32 Log on to av2books.com

Where in the World?

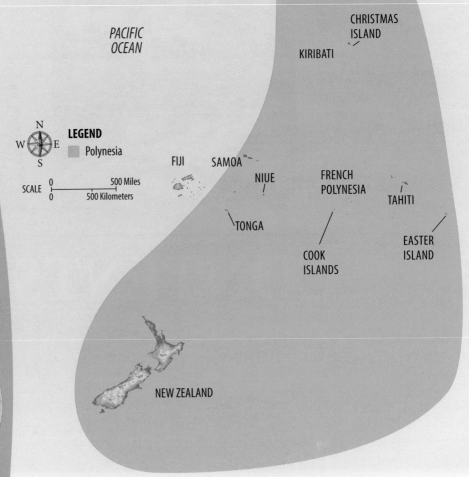

PACIFIC OCEAN

HAWAI'IAN ISLANDS

CHRISTMAS ISLAND

KIRIBATI

LEGEND
▢ Polynesia

N W E S

SCALE 0 ——— 500 Miles
0 ——— 500 Kilometers

FIJI

SAMOA

NIUE

FRENCH POLYNESIA

TAHITI

TONGA

COOK ISLANDS

EASTER ISLAND

NEW ZEALAND

ASIA

PACIFIC OCEAN

INDIAN OCEAN

AUSTRALIA

NEW ZEALAND

ANTARCTICA

Population: more than 10 million
Region: Oceania
Major Islands of Polynesia: Cook Islands, Easter Island, French Polynesia, Hawai'ian Islands, Kiribati, Marquesas Islands, New Zealand (Aotearoa), Samoa, Tonga
Area of Oceania: 317,700 square miles (822,843 square kilometers)

Thousands of years ago, a group of people set sail from Southeast Asia. They hoped to find a new land on which to settle. Riding aboard large canoes with no equipment to **navigate**, these brave people, called the Polynesians, became one of the **indigenous peoples** of the Pacific Islands.

Located off the coast of Southeast Asia, the Pacific Islands are a group of thousands of small islands. There is no exact count of how many islands are in the waters of the Pacific Ocean, but it is believed there are as many as 30,000. The Pacific Islands are often grouped into three main **culture** areas: Melanesia, Micronesia, and Polynesia. Polynesia is a triangle of area that is larger than Melanesia and Micronesia combined. New Zealand, or Aotearoa, is the triangle's southwestern tip. Easter Island is the southeastern tip. The Hawai'ian Islands make up the northern tip.

The Pacific Islands are well known for their beautiful scenery. Many of the larger islands, such as Hawai'i and Aotearoa, have narrow coastal plains with volcanic mountains and plateaus rising from the coast.

The word *Polynesia* means "many islands." The Polynesian Islands, which include Aotearoa, the Cook Islands, Easter Island, French Polynesia, Hawai'i, Samoa, and Tonga, were created from volcanic activity.

The people who live on these islands are called Polynesians. They have created a unique culture based on their rich history, society, and beliefs.

Culture Cues

- The Pacific Ocean is the largest and deepest ocean on Earth. It covers more than one-third of Earth's surface and stretches about 12,400 miles (19,956 km) wide. The Pacific Islands are scattered throughout this ocean.

- The islands of Aotearoa, Hawai'i, and New Guinea account for 93 percent of the land area of the Pacific Islands.

- The Pacific Islands, including Melanesia, Micronesia, and Polynesia, are also known as Oceania.

- Polynesia covers 5,000 miles (8,047 km) of the Pacific Ocean, from Hawai'i to Easter Island to Aotearoa.

Stories and Legends

Polynesians tell stories that celebrate their connection to the natural world. Many stories include themes of friendship, love, and loyalty.

In order to understand or explain their surroundings, the Polynesians created many stories and legends. Many of their beliefs are different from those of modern societies. For example, the Polynesians tell a unique story to explain how the universe was created. Traditional Polynesians believed that four **elements** were involved in the creation of the universe. The first element was the "world egg," which was thought to contain the seed of all living beings. The second element was the "nothingness" from which Earth was made. The Creator, named Ta'aroa, was the third element. The fourth element was a belief that Earth and Heaven are the source of all life in the universe. When combined, these four elements form a story of creation that Polynesians have passed on to younger **generations** for thousands of years. Depending on which island they live, Polynesian groups tell different versions of the story. However, each version usually contains the four elements.

The most feared god in Hawai'i was Pele, the goddess of volcanoes.

The ancient Polynesians were very **spiritual** people, and they believed in many gods. They believed these gods created the world and that the gods affected all events that happen on Earth.

Gods who were of great importance to the Polynesians included Tane, the god of light, Oro or Tu, the god of war, Rongo, the god of agriculture and peace, and Maui, the god of fire and fishing. Often, stone sculptures were carved to represent these gods. These statues were called *tiki*. They were honored by the Polynesians.

Sacred sites where the Polynesians gathered to worship the gods were called *marae*. Marae were large stone structures built in the open air, away from villages.

Polynesians carved stone sculptures called tiki to represent their gods.

THE STORY OF
How Maui Caught the Sun

One day, Hina, Maui's mother, told her son that she did not have enough time each day to complete her chores. She told Maui that if the Sun slowed its movement through the sky, there would be more daylight hours and she could tend to more of her daily duties.

Maui wanted to help his mother. He hid behind the highest mountain peak and waited for the Sun to pass overhead. He lassoed the Sun with a rope as it sped by. Before Maui released the Sun, he made it promise to slow down. The Sun promised to slow its passage through the sky.

Today, the mountain is known as *Haleakala*, which means "House of Sun." This mountain is located on the island of Maui in Hawai'i. On Maui, the days are always long and full of sunlight.

Out of the Past

The Polynesians began moving to the Pacific Islands about 3,000 years ago. They started settling the islands to the east of Australia. The first settlements were on the islands of Samoa and Tonga. Some of the Polynesians moved east to other islands as the population grew. They settled on the Marquesas Islands and Easter Island. Eventually, they began moving west until they reached the island of Aotearoa.

The Polynesians sailed across the Pacific Ocean in canoes they carved from tree trunks. The Polynesians did not use a map or compass. Instead, they used natural landmarks to help guide them. They observed their surroundings and tried to remember how the ocean, sky, or clouds appeared from different islands. The way the Sun lit parts of the landscape, or where the Sun would rise and set, were all clues that helped guide the crew safely to their destination. If their canoes did not sail along easily with the winds, the crew would paddle against **currents**. Canoes could withstand voyages longer than 2,000 miles (3,219 km).

Voyaging to the Pacific Islands was not an easy trip for these first settlers. Fierce winds, jagged rocks, and rough waters could destroy their canoes, **capsizing** the entire crew. Aside from holding several families, the canoes carried items such as food, livestock, seeds, and water. Some Polynesians ran out of food

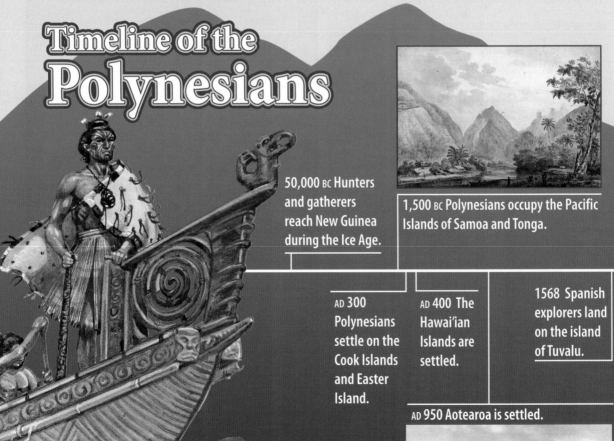

Timeline of the Polynesians

50,000 BC Hunters and gatherers reach New Guinea during the Ice Age.

1,500 BC Polynesians occupy the Pacific Islands of Samoa and Tonga.

AD 300 Polynesians settle on the Cook Islands and Easter Island.

AD 400 The Hawai'ian Islands are settled.

1568 Spanish explorers land on the island of Tuvalu.

AD 950 Aotearoa is settled.

and died of starvation before reaching land. From the first settled island to the last, it was about 1,000 years before the Pacific Islands were inhabited by the Polynesians.

Using natural resources found on the islands, the Polynesians adapted to their new surroundings. Their society started by fishing and farming. Once settled, the Polynesians **transplanted** seeds they had brought from their former homes. The Polynesians did not know about other countries or cultures. Similarly, the Europeans did not know about the Polynesian peoples living on the Pacific Islands.

The Europeans did not discover the Pacific Islands until the 1500s. By this time, Polynesian societies had already occupied the islands. The Europeans were amazed to learn that the Polynesians were able to sail to the islands without large sailing ships, navigational tools, or modern **technology**. For years, European explorers tried to explain how the Polynesians arrived and settled on the Pacific Islands. The first European to see the eastern shore of the Pacific Ocean was Spanish explorer Vasco Núñez de Balboa in 1513. Seven years later, Portuguese explorer Ferdinand Magellan became the first person to sail the Pacific Ocean. In 1769, Captain James Cook, a British explorer, visited one of the islands of Tahiti for four months. During this time, Captain Cook learned how to speak Polynesian. He also found out how the Polynesians came to inhabit the islands and how they were able to survive.

1778 Captain James Cook visits the island of Hawai'i.

1941 Japan bombs Pearl Harbor, Hawai'i, during World War II.

1945 World War II ends.

1996 France ends its nuclear testing program.

2004 France grants greater independence to French Polynesia.

1779 Captain Cook is killed in a fight.

1942 The Japanese capture the Pacific Islands.

1945 Japan surrenders the Pacific Islands and leaves.

1966 Tuamotus is the location of France's first test nuclear bomb explosion.

1797 **Protestant missionaries** enter the Polynesian area.

1950s The United States begins testing nuclear weapons on many of the Pacific Islands.

Social Structures

Finding food was the main work of Polynesians. Polynesian men spearfished at night using torches to lure the fish within reach.

The ancient Polynesians had very strict **rank systems** that were ruled by chiefs. On most of the Pacific Islands, the rank system had two main classes of people—chiefs and **commoners**. Usually the commoners farmed the land, which was often controlled by chiefs and their families. The chiefs would distribute the land's produce among the workers. There were other classes above commoners. These included experts such as boat-builders, healers, navigators, and priests.

On some islands, the land was owned equally by all members of the community. The location of the land determined how it would be used. The Polynesians who lived inland farmed to produce the food they needed to survive. Those who lived on the coast would fish. Both inland and coastal Polynesians added to their diets by eating fruits and other plant life. Producing and finding food was the main work of the Polynesians. Men were responsible for **spearfishing**, gardening, and building. Women would cook, weave, and gather plants for food. Aside from fishing and growing crops, Polynesians also raised pigs and chickens.

Crops planted on traditional Polynesian farms included taro, sweet potatoes, breadfruit, coconut, bananas, and sugarcane.

Traditionally, several generations of a family would live together in one house. Today, most households have fewer people, but family ties are still strong.

Family life was very important to the Polynesians. They often had large families with many children. Aunts, uncles, grandparents, and cousins had very close relationships. When family members would voyage to another island, the remaining family worried about the safety of the travelers. To ease their worries, a piece of coconut skin was passed under the travelers' canoe before it set sail. The coconut skin was then placed under a rock. It was removed only when the worried family members felt their traveling relatives should have reached their destination. They observed the condition of the shriveled coconut skin. They believed that its condition could tell them whether their loved ones had survived the voyage. There is still a sense of community among Polynesian societies. Often, Polynesians gather to perform a ceremony or help with a community project.

THE TWO SEASONS

There are two seasons on the Pacific Islands—wet and dry. On most of the islands, the wet season is between December and March. **Typhoons** often strike the islands between January and March. They can cause great damage, such as the loss of life and property. The dry season is between April and November. On most of the islands, the temperature does not drop below 70° Fahrenheit (21°C) or rise above 80°F (27°C).

Communication

When the Polynesians first settled on the Pacific Islands, they had no written language. Instead, they would memorize **chants**. These chants were sometimes used as stories, teachings, or even directions. When the Polynesians traveled to another island, there were no written maps for them to follow. To aid their voyage, they sang chants to describe the birds, clouds, current, water color, winds, and the position of the Sun. These chants served as the Polynesians' only record of directions to other islands. They relied on memory. If they did not memorize these chants before they set out for another island, they might become lost. The chants and stories of the Polynesians were handed down to their **kin**. Sometimes, they placed objects, such as bamboo sticks, pebbles, or shells, in special arrangements on tree bark. This was often done to show travelers the

MOKO

Moko are detailed tattoos that cover the face and body. For some Polynesian communities, moko did not have a special meaning. They were simply used to create attractive patterns. For other communities, moko represented bravery and one's ability to endure great pain.

Moko were also used as a form of communication. People with detailed location of the other islands. They would also arrange objects to describe the direction the wind was blowing as they were traveling.

Often, young Polynesian boys memorized ceremonies, events, and stories. The boys would remember these events in order to pass the story along to future generations. The Polynesians called these boys "memory keepers." Without memory keepers, there would be no record of Polynesian history.

Today, there are about 20 different Polynesian languages. These languages are closely related. English is the official language on most Polynesian islands, but many indigenous peoples still speak their native language.

Singing and dancing were the main forms of communication in traditional Polynesian culture. Polynesians would often sing and dance to welcome visitors.

moko were usually feared leaders and chiefs. During battles, facial moko would communicate to opposing villages which warrior was the group's leader.

Moko also tell the story of a person's life. They show their age, bravery, social status, and wealth.

Law and Order

Polynesians often performed ceremonial dances to thank the gods or honor important leaders.

The ancient Polynesians were very spiritual people. Their lives were **governed** by two forces—*mana* and *tapu*. Mana was a spiritual power. Anyone with mana was held in high regard and given respect. These people helped rule Polynesian life. The other force that governed Polynesian life was tapu. Tapu means "taboo," which is something forbidden by society. The Polynesians had many taboos that guided their everyday life. For example, commoners were banned from using certain plants. These plants were to be used by the chiefs only. It was tapu for commoners to touch these plants. On some islands, it was tapu for the highest chiefs, or chiefs with mana, to come in contact with commoners.

Polynesian society was very structured. It was believed that the gods and chiefs had the most mana, and the commoners had the least mana. The commoners lived in constant fear of the gods. The village chief was an important person in Polynesian societies. The chief was expected to

advise and lead the villagers in their everyday activities. The chief would also act as a host to visitors. Usually, men who became village chiefs were given the honor because their father had been the village chief. This honor was passed down from one generation to the next.

In most modern Polynesian communities, chiefs no longer have this much power. On some islands, chiefs are still held in high regard and live in the traditional social structures of their ancestors.

King Kamehameha I was a very powerful Hawai'ian ruler who helped unite the Hawai'ian islands. Statues of him are found throughout Hawai'i.

Celebrating Culture

Although Polynesians live on many different islands, they often view themselves as a group of people from the same culture, just as other early societies once did.

The early Polynesians learned to survive in their new surroundings. In the beginning, their culture was faced with a problem. They lived in an unfavorable environment. Some areas of the islands were too harsh for the Polynesians to settle. Other areas were rainforest. Regions of volcanic ash or ocean inlets were not suitable for farming. The lack of workable land forced the Polynesians to live close together where the land was most suitable. This created a tightly woven society and culture. The Polynesians farmed the land for their survival. Every food item the Polynesians ate or produced came from the environment.

As a result, land became an important part of their culture and was a part of their religious ceremonies. The Polynesians knew that gardens must be tended and food had to be prepared. Unlike many of today's societies, they did not earn money by working for a set number of hours each day. They would work long, hard hours until daily tasks were complete. They were not paid for their work. Still, different Polynesian communities would trade items. On an island, those who lived inland often provided those living near the coast with land products, such as fruits.

Even today, the land is an important part of Polynesian culture. May farmers harvest taro, a root vegetable.

In return, Polynesians living on the coast gave fish from the sea to those who lived inland. This trading system ensured all Polynesian communities had the resources they needed to survive.

The Polynesians lived in huts made from natural resources. Tall bamboo poles were placed side-by-side in a circle in the ground. Thin bamboo poles were placed on top to support a **thatched** roof. The huts protected the Polynesians from frequent rains and the hot Sun. Many Polynesians still live in this type of house.

Even before the Europeans arrived on the Pacific Islands, the Polynesians would travel between the islands. They traveled to other islands for many reasons. Sometimes, Polynesians traveled to other islands in search of a husband or wife. Other times, a person would return to the island where he or she was born to visit family members. This type of visiting helped to spread and maintain the Polynesian culture among the islanders.

Ceremonies remain an important part of Polynesian culture. Many groups still gather to attend births, funerals, and weddings. Some wear traditional Polynesian clothing and perform cultural rituals.

Like their ancestors, Polynesians use products grown or made on their home islands. However, they also enjoy trade goods from all over the world.

Huts with thatched roofs protected Polynesians from the rain and hot sun.

Art and Culture

The most common form of art for Polynesian groups was dancing. The Polynesians used dancing to tell stories. *Hula* dancing is one type of dance still performed on the islands of Hawai'i. Hula means "dance." Dancers swing their hips to musical beats and sway their arms to tell a story, legend, or describe the beauty of the Pacific Islands. Teachers of the hula dance are called *kumu*. Hula dancing is often performed to the music of stringed instruments such as the **ukulele** or the guitar.

There are many forms of Polynesian dance. Each dance may tell a unique story about Polynesian culture. Some tell the story of Earth's creation. Others tell stories about heroes and chiefs.

Ancient rock carvings show the birdman image that was sacred to the Polynesians of Easter Island.

On the Cook Islands, the art of dance is also a very important part of the Polynesian culture. On these islands, children are taught to dance at a young age. They are expected to practice these dances often. They perform the *hura* dance, which is similar to the hula. Dancers often compete against one another to show their skill. In Tahiti, one of the most popular dances performed during feasts and celebrations is the *tamure*. The tamure is a quick dance that is similar to the hula.

As with many indigenous groups, baskets were a common necessity used to hold items. The Polynesians became quite skilled at making baskets. Using fibers or long leaves from plants or nearby trees, the Polynesians would braid or knot the fibers into long strips. These long strips were woven into baskets that were used to carry items. Other objects that the Polynesians would weave included cloth, mats, and sandals. Many Polynesians still practice these traditional art forms.

Polynesians weave strips of palm leaves together to make floor mats, baskets, and even walls or roofs for traditional houses.

Stone Gods

Carving is a popular art form practiced on the Pacific Islands. Usually, the image of a Polynesian god is carved in stone or wood. The representations are called tiki. Some tiki are small carvings on the handle of a comb or fan. Others are large stone sculptures or wooden posts. Tiki are often found in sacred areas where the Polynesians gathered to honor the gods.

Dressing Up

Some Polynesians still dress in the same style of clothing that was worn by their ancestors. Both men and women may wear a *sulu*. A sulu is a piece of cloth that is wrapped around the waist in the same style as a skirt. Since the weather on the islands is very hot, the fabric of a sulu is lightweight. Traditional clothes are most often worn during important events, such as weddings or funerals. Some Polynesians continue to wear these items every day.

Ancient Polynesian women often used a type of cloth called *tapa* to make their clothing. Tapa is made from tree bark. The inner bark of a mulberry tree is stripped, soaked, and pounded repeatedly to make a soft, thick cloth. Ancient Polynesians used coral limestone to pound the cloth. The rough limestone sometimes left a design on the cloth. Today, ancient **templates** and stamps are used to decorate the cloth. Pounding the strips of cloth makes them larger and wider. These strips also stick together to make larger pieces of cloth. Tapa cloth is still made on the Pacific Islands. It is often used for bedding, clothing, home decorations, and tablecloths.

Tattooing was once a popular custom in Polynesian culture. Tattoos were a sign of beauty. Both men and women practiced this custom, but it was more important for a man to be tattooed. Combs, made of bone or tortoise shells with hard teeth on the handle, were used to make tattoos. The person drawing

A sulu can be worn as a beach wrap or as a skirt.

the tattoo would lightly hammer the comb into the skin with a small **mallet**. To color the tattoo, an oily fruit called a *kukui nut* was put on skewers, or long sticks, and burned to produce **soot**. The soot was then applied to the skin. Each island community had different tattoo patterns. Some of the patterns included animals, horizontal bands, and human shapes. Tattooing is once again becoming an important part of Polynesian culture. It helps Polynesians maintain a part of their culture and history.

Polynesians today continue to create tattoos in the same way their ancestors did.

Tapa, or bark cloth, is made from tree bark. Dyes of different colors are applied to the bark to create pleasing designs.

LACING LEIS

Leis are necklaces made from bone, feathers, plants, and shells that have been braided, twisted, or woven together. In early times, Polynesians wore leis to make themselves more beautiful. They also offered leis to the gods during special ceremonies. They gave leis to one another as a symbol of love and friendship. Today, leis are most commonly made from colorful and **fragrant** flowers.

Though leis are a traditional part of Polynesian culture, they have become popular with other societies. For example, tourists visiting the Hawai'ian Islands are greeted with a floral lei. According to legend, tourists should toss their leis into the ocean before they leave the islands. If the lei floats to shore, it means that the person will return to the islands one day.

Food and Fun

During voyages, it was important for the Polynesians to have a healthy source of nutritious foods. While traveling the vast waters of the Pacific Ocean, the early Polynesians ate seabirds as one of their main food sources. Prior to their journey, they would preserve and **ferment** foods such as bananas and yams. These foods, along with fish, provided a healthy diet during their long travels.

Once settled on their new land, they continued to eat fish and plants. The Polynesians would also fish for crabs, lobsters, shrimp, and even turtles. If they voyaged out to sea, sometimes they would catch tuna. On land, Polynesians ate bananas, **cassava**, papayas, sweet potatoes, taros, and yams.

Coconuts were also an important food in the Polynesian diet. Meat from a coconut was a main food source. Coconut milk was a tasty drink. Once eaten, the shell of a coconut was used as a bowl, a cup, or a drum to make music. Coconut oil was used for cooking and waterproofing canoes.

In order to cook food, the Polynesians made an underground oven called an *imu*. To make an imu, they would dig a shallow hole or pit in the ground. A layer of heated rocks was placed on the bottom of the pit. Food was put on top of the rocks and then covered with a layer of leaves.

Polynesian Diet

Polynesians traditionally ate a varied diet of animal and plant foods.

Kumara • Bananas • Watermelon • Crabs • Pigs • Tuna • Coconut • Sea Turtles

Fruits and Vegetables
Seafood
Red Meat
Reptiles

Imus are used to prepare traditional foods for people visiting Polynesia.

Another layer of hot rocks and leaves was placed on top of the food. Finally, the pit was filled with dirt. Later, the cooked food was removed from the imu and eaten.

Many traditional ways of preparing Polynesian foods are still practiced. Some communities also grow **foreign** vegetables, such as tomatoes. Many eat processed foods that come from other countries.

For fun, early Polynesians held ceremonies filled with dancing, feasting, and music. **Gourds** were used as rattles or hollowed out to make small drums. Trumpets were made from conch shells found along the coast. The Polynesians would blow into the tip of these large seashells to make a loud, low sound. Bamboo shoots were used to make small flutes. While the music played, Polynesians would dance and sing.

In addition to dancing and feasting, today some Polynesians play sports for fun. Many of these sports were created in Western countries. They include volleyball and rugby. Surfing is also a very popular sport on the islands. The Polynesians invented this sport more than 3,000 years ago when they stood on wooden boards in the surf of the Pacific Ocean.

Shredded Coconut Recipe

- Preheat oven to 250°F.
- Ask an adult to use a mallet to break open a coconut.
- Pour the coconut milk into a glass.
- Use a scraper, or a tool with teeth or sharp edges, to scrape the coconut meat from the inner shell.
- Shred the meat to a fine texture using a grater or food processor.
- Spread coconut on baking sheet.
- Bake for 15 minutes or until dry and brittle to the touch. Remove from oven when it begins to brown.
- Sprinkle the coconut on top of brownies, sundaes, or other desserts.

Great Ideas

Using natural resources, the Polynesians created some unique items. From developing tools to survive on the land to building ocean crafts, the Polynesians found many ways to ensure their culture continued.

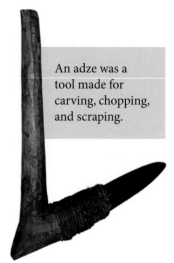

An adze was a tool made for carving, chopping, and scraping.

Since the Polynesians did not have matches, they made fire by quickly rubbing pieces of wood together. This was not an easy task. It took time and patience to make a fire. To help the process, they made a "fire saw." Using this tool, they were able to create the fire they needed to cook their food as well as provide light and heat.

The Polynesians needed tools to cut, carve, and scrape. They made sharp tools for cutting called *adzes*. Adzes were made from basalt, bone, coral, or stone. Basalt is a very hard, volcanic rock found on many Pacific Islands. Adzes were used to chop trees or slice fish. When an adze became dull, the Polynesians would rub it on sandstone to sharpen it.

The Polynesians used adzes to build a special type of *wa'a*, or canoe, that would not tip over in the water. Using an adze, the Polynesians hollowed out a large log. This formed the hull, or frame, of the canoe. Often, a second log was hollowed out and fastened along the length of the first using timber crossbeams. This increased the canoe's stability in rough waters. To help stabilize single-hull canoes, an **outrigger** was attached to one side of the hull. An outrigger was attached to both

Polynesians attached an outrigger to the hull of their canoes to make them more stable on the sea.

sides of a double-hull canoe. A platform was placed on top of the crossbeams. This provided passengers with a place to live during their voyage.

One person sat at the front of the canoe to steer. He used a rope and a short stick to steer the canoe through the water. This was similar to a **rudder** on modern sailing ships. Sails made from matting also helped steer the canoe. Winds blew through the sails, moving the canoe forward.

Sometimes long, flat pieces of wood were sewn together, with twisted coconut fibers to add strength to the canoes. The canoes were about 60 feet (18 m) long. They could carry about 24 people as well as animals, food, plants, and supplies.

Since these canoes had no navigational instruments, the Polynesians used the stars to guide their progress. Polynesian travelers used a tool called a latitude hook to measure the distance between a star and the horizon. The measurement of this distance helped the navigator determine how far north or south he was.

When making a canoe, Polynesians used an adze to hollow out the trunk of a tree.

The Fire Starter

To make a fire saw, a cut was made in the center of a piece of dry softwood. A hard piece of wood was placed upright inside the cut. This hard piece of wood was sawed, or rubbed, back and forth quickly. Rubbing caused some of the wood to become **tinder**, or sawdust. This rubbing action also made the tinder **smolder**. Fanning the smoldering tinder would spark a flame, which would become a fire.

At Issue

Some Pacific Islands are popular places for tourists to visit. However, tourism may cause environmental problems and spoil the natural beauty of the beaches.

Increased contact with Europeans and other Western societies have caused the Polynesians concern about the current state of their environment. Some issues of importance include global warming, overfishing, and the breakdown of the **ozone layer**. Also, prepackaged food products are causing health problems for these indigenous peoples.

Global warming may cause severe problems for islanders. Some scientists believe that an increase in greenhouse gases is causing Earth's temperature to rise. If this continues, ice on mountains around the world will begin to melt. The melting ice will flow into the sea. As a result, water levels will rise. This would cause disaster for many Polynesian communities. They would lose some of their shorelines, and the rising ocean might entirely cover some islands, such as Tonga.

The breakdown of Earth's ozone layer also causes concern for the Polynesians. The ozone layer protects living things from the Sun's harmful rays. Recently, a hole has formed in this protective layer. Rays are coming through this hole.

Native Hawai'ians become politically active when development threatens the environment.

This is a problem for the Polynesians because the Sun is closer to the Pacific Islands than any other region on Earth. Severe burns or cancers caused by these rays can harm the Polynesians. This was not an issue when the Polynesians' ancestors settled on the Pacific Islands thousands of years ago.

Since foreign foods, such as imported chicken parts and lamb belly, have been available on the Pacific Islands, **malnutrition** has become a concern in many cities and towns. These canned and prepackaged foods require less effort to prepare than traditional foods, but they are also less healthy. Eating such foods is causing more Polynesians to develop **diabetes**. Many others are lacking vitamins. As well, large fishing fleets from neighboring countries have **depleted** the number of fish in the Pacific Ocean. As a result, there are fewer fish for the Polynesians to catch and eat.

Native Hawai'ian Sovereignty Movement

In the 1960s, native Hawai'ians started a civil rights movement to help preserve their culture. In 1976, the group staged small protests against the U.S. military who used the area of Kaho'olawe as a testing site for bombs. In 1993, the U.S. government stopped using the site for bombing practice. It also issued a formal apology for illegally overthrowing the Kingdom of Hawai'i in January 1893.

The Native Hawai'ian Sovereignty Movement combines about 40 indigenous groups who live throughout the islands. Each group seeks to preserve the islands. For example, one group wants all non-native Hawai'ians removed from the islands. They also want to prevent others from moving to the islands. Still, most groups hope to find a practical solution to the problems facing their people.

Into the Future

Many Polynesians eat the same foods, live in the same type of houses, and wear the same style of clothing as their ancestors. Still, this is beginning to change. Since many other countries have brought their culture to the Pacific Islands, some Polynesians have adapted their way of life to include foreign culture. Many Polynesians who live in cities now work in factories, offices, or as salespeople, for example.

It is difficult for the Polynesians to choose between their traditional culture and modern society. By choosing to live as part of a modern society, the Polynesians can benefit from educational resources, new fishing and farming techniques, health services, and improved transportation. In exchange, they may give up many of their cultural traditions.

Today, some Polynesians are trying to rediscover their **heritage**. They are fascinated by stories about their **ancestors'** travels to the Pacific Islands. The Polynesian Voyaging Society (PVS) was formed in 1973. PVS members aim to retrace the movements of their ancestors as they sailed to the Pacific Islands. Members have reconstructed their ancestors' ancient canoes from natural resources. They have sailed across the waters of the Pacific Ocean following the same route their ancestors traveled. By doing this, the Polynesians are rediscovering their heritage. They are also learning about how difficult it was for their ancestors to reach the islands. Recreating the journey from beginning to end might help younger generations understand the culture of the early Polynesians. Since 1973, more than 500,000 people have participated in PVS programs.

Polynesian children participate in traditional ceremonies to learn about their cultural heritage.

Role-play Debate

When people debate a topic, two sides take a different viewpoint about one idea. Each side presents logical arguments to support its views. In a role-play debate, participants act out the roles of the key people or groups involved with the different viewpoints. Role-playing can build communication skills and help people understand how others may think and feel. Usually, each person or team is given a set amount of time to present its case. The participants take turns stating their arguments until the time set aside for the debate is up.

THE ISSUE

In 1893, the U.S. government overthrew the legal government of Hawai'i. Hawai'i was annexed by the United States, and in 1959 it became a state. In 1993, the U.S. Congress apologized for the overthrow and annexation and acknowledged that it was illegal. Today, some native Hawai'ians favor total independence for Hawai'i as the best way to restore their culture. Some non-native Hawai'ians fear that native Hawai'ians would control the land and hold most of the political power in an independent Hawai'i.

THE QUESTION

Should Hawai'i be granted independence and be recognized as a sovereign nation by the U.S. government?

THE SIDES

NO

Non-native Hawai'ians: Hawai'i became a state in 1959 through a fair, democratic process. Hawai'ian statehood should not be dissolved by a vocal minority. In an independent Hawai'i, non-natives would not enjoy equal rights with native Hawai'ians.

YES

Native Hawai'ians: The annexation of Hawai'i by the U.S. government was illegal. It is only fair and just that our nation be returned to us and our independence be restored.

Ready, Set, Go

Form two teams to debate the issue, and decide whether your team will play the role of the native Hawai'ians or the role of the non-native Hawai'ians. Each team should use this book and other research to develop solid arguments for its side and to understand how the issue affects each group. At the end of the role-play debate, discuss how you feel after hearing both points of view.

World Cultures Quiz!

1 What does the name *Polynesia* mean?

2 According to Polynesian beliefs, what was the first element in the creation of the universe?

3 What is the name for sacred sites where Polynesians gathered to worship their gods?

4 At about what time did Polynesians begin to settle in the Pacific Islands?

5 When is the wet season on most Pacific Islands?

6 How did Polynesians preserve their history?

7 What are *tiki*?

8 What is the name for necklaces of feathers, flowers, and shells that are given as a symbol of friendship?

9 What was the purpose of an outrigger on a canoe?

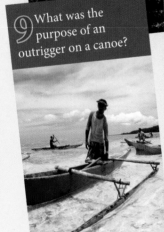

10 How might global warming affect islands throughout the Pacific?

ANSWER KEY

1. many islands **2.** the world egg **3.** marae **4.** about 3,000 years ago **5.** between December and March **6.** through "memory keepers," or boys who memorized ceremonies, events, and stories **7.** carvings in stone or wood, usually of a Polynesian god **8.** leis **9.** It helped to stabilize the canoe. **10.** Rising sea levels might cover shorelines or entire islands.

Key Words

ancestors people from the past who are related to modern people

capsizing overturning by accident

cassava a plant with large roots, used to make a type of flour

chants simple songs

commoners people who do not have a high social class

culture the customs, traditions, and values of a nation or people

currents moving waters

depleted reduced in size or amount

diabetes a disease caused when the body cannot control the amount of sugar in the blood

elements parts of something

ferment chemical change caused by a living substance, such as yeast

foreign belonging to another country

fragrant a pleasant scent

generations people of the same age living in a society or family

gourds round or bottle-shaped fruit with hard shells that are not eaten

governed ruled or controlled

heritage the traditions, language, and customs of a culture from the past

indigenous peoples the first, or original, inhabitants of a region or country

kin family members or relatives

mallet hammer with a large, flat side made of wood or rubber

malnutrition poor health caused by a poor diet

navigate to direct which way an object will travel

outrigger a float that is used to balance a canoe

ozone layer a layer of air above Earth that prevents the Sun's harmful rays from reaching Earth

Protestant missionaries people sent by a non-Catholic Christian church to carry out the work of the church

rank systems ways to group people based on their importance in society

rudder wood or metal on the back of a boat that is moved from side to side to change direction

sacred spiritual, religious, or holy

smolder to burn slowly

soot a black powder produced when something is burned

spearfishing using a spear to catch fish instead of a hook and line

spiritual a religious word for the soulful part of a person that is not part of the body

technology scientific discoveries that aid everyday life

templates a pattern that is used to make shapes on another object

thatched roof covering made from straw and reeds

tinder small pieces of a dry material, such as wood, used to start a fire

transplanted the process of taking something from one place and moving it to another location

typhoons strong winds that occur in the Western Pacific Ocean

ukulele an instrument that looks like a small guitar and has four strings

Index

ancestors 15, 17, 20, 27, 28
Aotearoa 4, 5, 8

Captain James Cook 9
chants 12
chiefs 10, 13, 14, 15, 18
commoners 10, 14
Cook Islands 4, 5, 8, 19

dancing 13, 14, 18, 19, 23

Easter Island 4, 5, 8, 18
environment 16, 26
Europeans 9, 17, 26

farming 9, 10, 16, 28
fire 7, 24, 25
fishing 7, 9, 10, 22, 27, 28
food 8, 10, 16, 22, 23, 24, 25, 26, 27, 28
French Polynesia 4, 5, 9

gods 7, 14, 19, 21, 30
government 27, 29

Hawai'i 4, 5, 6, 7, 8, 9, 15, 18, 21, 27, 29

Marquesas Islands 4, 8
Melanesia 4, 5
Micronesia 4, 5
music 18, 22, 23

ozone layer 26

Pacific Islands 4, 5, 8, 9, 10, 11, 12, 17, 18, 19, 20, 24, 26, 27, 28, 30
Pacific Ocean 4, 5, 8, 9, 22, 23, 27, 28

spearfishing 10

Ta'aroa 6
tapa cloth 20, 21
tapu 14
tiki 7, 19, 30

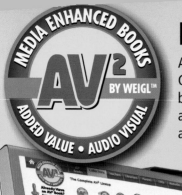

Log on to www.av2books.com

AV² by Weigl brings you media enhanced books that support active learning. Go to www.av2books.com, and enter the special code found on page 2 of this book. You will gain access to enriched and enhanced content that supplements and complements this book. Content includes video, audio, weblinks, quizzes, a slide show, and activities.

Audio
Listen to sections of the book read aloud.

Video
Watch informative video clips.

Embedded Weblinks
Gain additional information for research.

Try This!
Complete activities and hands-on experiments.

WHAT'S ONLINE?

Try This!	Embedded Weblinks	Video	EXTRA FEATURES
Map the area in which the Polynesians live.	Learn more about the Polynesians.	Watch a video of Polynesian dancing.	**Audio** Listen to sections of the book read aloud.
Write a biography about a well-known Polynesian.	Read about the history of the Polynesians.	See how the Polynesians live today.	**Key Words** Study vocabulary, and complete a matching word activity.
Create a timeline showing the history of the Polynesians.	View the arts and crafts of the Polynesians.		**Slide Show** View images and captions, and prepare a presentation.
Draw a chart to show the foods the Polynesians eat.			**Quizzes** Test your knowledge.
Test your knowledge of the Polynesians.			

AV² was built to bridge the gap between print and digital. We encourage you to tell us what you like and what you want to see in the future.

Sign up to be an AV² Ambassador at www.av2books.com/ambassador.